HELLFIRES
SHAKE THE BLUES

A Bar Bible
of
Poetry

Peter Jacob Streitz

Copyright © 2015 Peter Jacob Streitz
All rights reserved

ISBN 13: 9798743224739

For Donna

IN MEMORY OF RICHARD PRYOR

Contents

A DYING MOTHER

It was a joyous occasion.
Not for me.
Nor her.
But the football star
in the next room over.
The one
with the cheerleaders
beaming over his bed.
Shaking their pom-poms.
While dorky friends
wished they were him;
with a broken ankle
and winning touchdown.
Just their shouts
of joy
or infantile whispers
made me
want to murder them.
Or at least,
make them suffer—
on this bright fall
day . . .
as my mother lay
dying . . .
in her hospital bed.
Wrapped in her religion.
Moving away from me.

Holding hands
with another.
Like a first time date.
Shyly dancing
to his touch.
Leaving no space
to cut in.
Or request . . .
our song.
She was going home
with him.
As teammates
laughed
and girlfriends
tittered
I watched her
leave the prom—
to the chorus
. . . of youth . . .
. . . I rejoiced . . .
in their oblivion;
while muting the truth
—that the strains
of this measure—
were not yet theirs
to share.
For that note
. . . eternally plays . . .
far too soon.

2

MLK

I'm no longer MLK
or Mahatma.
Hell, I'm not even Robert
Kennedy.
Much less Jack.
And forget Harriet Tubman.
All I wanted was . . .
the prize.
The peace
and justice.
For all those years
of fighting my past
and presenting myself
as open to every change
—and hoping—
my former Being
could be forgiven
for transgressions
. . . not of my doing . . .
but in my nature;
while the saintliness
of my new design
desired to be
the low hanging fruit
lynched high in penitence
. . . swaying from a tree . . .

that sprinkles liberally
my seeds
of struggle . . .
goodness and light
. . . on an earth
ripe with new dawns—
that pierce the darkness
with an awakening
sunshine.
Yet the world—
blinded by this virtue
—turned tiredly away.
Denying the angelic
sowing
of a heart unrestrained;
progressively collapsing
the morrow
with realities
etched in stone
from the bad old days.

THE GOTHAM BEETLE

Her chrysalis
forever lies
beneath
stacks of human debris
and animal waste.
Plus, truckloads
of asphalt
and concrete—
while rising
rumbles of smoke
and steam
escape subway grates
and joints
just lit . . .
send straight shots
of excitement,
or dread,
down the veins
of Harlem . . .
and into the streets
most walled—
relentlessly tumbling
her turd balls
of nourishment,
and husbandry,
into the cribs
of tenements
and townhouses alike

... regenerating
her incessant bloat
with eggs
transplanted
from wistful women
and expectant men—
drawn by the pheromones
of fame and fortune
... or pure survival ...
as they seed
what's buried below
with frequencies
both national
and worldwide:
not as an alien
plague
but a renewal
of her brood
metamorphosing
into the larva
of production
and the pupa
of love.
Birthing arty
imagoes
of perpetual tension.
Exciting
... past understanding ...

with moonlit nights,
or days so bright,
that the pavement sears
with mirages
of diversity
and personal chic
so deep
and unforgiving
that Kings
wear work boots
and Queens dress
in off-the-rack
...seamlessly
blending the fabrics
of existence
into a richness
only the Scarabs
of Egyptian Gods
could fathom
...dreaming afresh...
this womb
of possibility.
Like earth Angels!
Wandering bravely beyond
even the cruelest
streets
of man's
most transformative
Shangri La.

DIANA

A white boy
watched
in amazement
on his black
and white TV . . .
the Medusa
seducing
Masters
of how things
were supposed to be.
With ugliness
nonexistent
and segregation
an unbearable stance,
she shimmied
a feminine eloquence
that retold . . .
a sequined dance
—of wrongs—
and misconception
through a smile
so sunny white
. . . it set fire . . .
to a darkness
that petrified
the night.
Like the hand
of motherly forgiveness
. . . she soothed

a soulful sin . . .
of sons sowing
supremacy
in a separating wind.
Spinning seeds
sent a-scattering
and spiraling
out of control
. . . showering
farms
and plantations
in storms
that took its toll.
Of rights
so wrong
that the land
distorted
in the spotlight
of the day . . .
sending sheaves
of inner vision
to strike
against
the play—
of those
so shadowy
nocturnal
that they seized
upon the fright
. . . riding
HIGH

along the apocalypse
while sheeted
by the night.
Like the cowardice
of specters
flying in full flee,
leaving fields
untilled
and others fallow
... awaiting ...
the rightful deed.
Delivering
a supreme
enlightenment
from the dimness
of the womb,
swaddled,
in the sentience
—here to spell—
the doom.
When screening
for the world
as one
—its essence—
fully blown
... executing
a deflowering
—to blossoms—
now dethroned.

SHAKESPEARE IN THE DARK

The tweeker's
boggy, alcoholic eyes
bulged unblinkingly
within inches of mine.
Setting the stage.
For mere players.
In this mosh pit
at the intersection of ol'Frisco
and modernity.
While the watery whirl
of rush hour washed 'round
and Dino denied I've come—
to that very corner
—every day—
for the past twenty years . . .
awaiting my love's return
from work.
But on this day,
where the subway
emerges
and the street cars clank
like ships
. . . passing in the night . . .
I unknowingly missed her
as she unknowingly missed me
but Dino didn't miss a beat

while manically orating
his resurrection
as a bookseller
. . . who only . . .
reads the law.
And fuck
that storytelling crap!
He spat . . .
as his countenance
became
increasingly
inscribed
with an ominous glaze
. . . lifting his lids
to half-mast,
he pulled back the curtain
—for the briefest moment—
to inquire . . .
do you read?
What?
There was no answer
other than his,
"Shakespeare."
Leading to
his sidewalk bibliothèque
where ten tomes of prose
sat dog-eared and dirty,
along with a soiled sleeping mat,
and a rat

disguised as a pet
entrapped beneath
a milk crate.
Much Ado About Nothing
was crammed into my hand
as two bucks
departed this fool
... from a wad of money ...
that filled Dino's head
with sugar plums of theft
or thirst for some complicity
whose outright criminality
got quenched with past drinks,
and blackouts,
at whore houses
in Alaska
and racist chases
in Texas by Rangers
who took exception
to the pilfering
of black velvet
bedspreads—
when shit and damn
my cell phone vibrated
and a distraught
wifely voice
rung down the curtain
on two role players
in another performance
of their life.

13

MISTER BROWN

The power of black
rushed the stage—
divined as a great
caped warrior . . .
sweating diamonds
that glistened
against a seashell
smile.
Sailing
across shores
of cotton white.
Leaving footprints
in the soils
of time
as he quick
. . . stepped
against
the devils
opposing
stones rolling
in backrooms
towards
frontmen
who vamped
their way
past every lock
and door.
Breaking down

the keys
to psyches
both harmful
and dear
while lines
of feminine
support
screamed
anthems
to his charge.
Never letting
the courage
flag or falter
as mamas
and daddies
desired
brand new swags
of ancestry
and grace.
Strengthened
by a troubadour
all funk.
And drums
creating
the base beat
of America's
Dream.

And possibilities.
In concert
with all others
. . . as a maestro . . .
of soulful
symphonies
drowning out
the riots
of men
against themselves.
For this moment
in time
. . . like a river
famously cresting
its banks . . .
to douse
the flames
in dignity
and brotherhood.
Only to have them
ignite again.

SNOWDEN . . .

idolized
the Monster.
Who laid lurking
in the weeds.
Eating power pills
of teleprompted
media.
Gaining strength—
and true believers.
As he promised
everybody
everything
and huffed
he'd never
take it away.
Oh, how they rejoiced!
Jumping on
and off wagons.
Beating the band.
And seeking . . .
his embrace.
Like the three blind
mice
chasing
the farmer's wife.
Their visions
of milk and honey
freely flowing

from the behemoth's
nurturing hand
was a dream
come true . . .
for all those hiding
in their holes
of security . . .
when a bastard
bug
stung the troll
with a toxin
of truth—
that buzzed about
the wonderland
in an epidemic
of uncertainty
and disbelief.
Forcing everyone
back to their nest;
to reinforce,
if not,
bar passage
to their portals
of sycophancy
and adulation
from the hand
once sworn
to feed them.

WINGED RATS

Bullshit!
Unless you consider
they eat the same crap.
But you'd be wrong.
These low flying
aviators
of the cityscape
got zip codes
and statues
and ordnances as white
as the driven snow.
In some hoods—
they're the only fauna
that doesn't attack
and kill
as ordered.
Or destroy the trees
with piss and shit.
And forget the grass.
Instead, these citizens
of aerial reconnaissance
clean up after bums
and partygoers.
Doing such civic duties
. . . as eating
the rice and beans
regurgitated

by soup kitchen
devotees.
Or their counterparts
boogying in
from bedroom
communities . . .
leaving their suburban
blight
for clean-up
by those living
aloft.
On the ledge.
With only one way
to fall.
Pilotless.
And no safety net.
Dying alone.
Earthbound.
In their mourning suits.
Having seen it all
on the toughest streets
. . . yet nothing . . .
of remembrance.
Not even the homage
of never more.

POETRY

It's a strange thing,
direct and to the point.
Or not at all.
It reminds one of ghost towns,
or maybe, a forgotten fort.
All around the battles rage.
Or dead silence hums.
Men long gone come again.
And the women of their dreams.
It shouts with life
and echoes of more;
bearing specters
that no one sees.
Meaning poetry of the heart
is crossed
with every view.

THAT NOT SAID

That not said tattooed his heart
with words of soulful ink.
That not said . . . means the world to him
as she brought him to the brink.
But time destroys this power
and life ignores the fact
of that not said
. . . unheeded . . .
turns the verities
all to black.
So all that speaks
—is muteness—
when love
is the truth be told.
That not said
. . . is the lone response . . .
as she packed in time to go.
Those cries for understanding
—as she writhed upon their bed—
were the final call to voice
"those words" he left unsaid.
So silence was his utterance
as she headed out the door,
and what he adored most in life
was lost with words no more.

BEAUTIFUL GIRLS

Same as the ugly
ones.
Except they carry
a package.
A burden.
Sometimes it's open.
Others it's closed.
Or empty.
Yet full of bows
and hair that styles
. . . a deep cut
cleavage.
With eyelashes
galore.
But forget the lips . . .
they're personal.
Carrying all kinds
of baggage.
With stickers
of exotic places.
And possibilities.
Of suitors lying
on hot sand
beaches
caressing a thigh
or curvaceous calf.

With palms
slick with lotion . . .
that never seals
the deal,
but adds
to the weight.
As it depletes it
of attractions,
and fades
. . . the horizons . . .
making the sights
too much
to bear.

THE CABOTS' FENCE

Will anger ever twist my mind
tight as the muscle
squeezing out
the known things—
from my years gone by?
Can I own
or control the things
in me . . .
my guts or heart?
My laughter or tears?
Where's utopia?
Is it under the broken street light
down in the gutter
or behind the Cabots' fence?
Near the pool?
I'm sure they have a pool;
my mother told me so.
Though I've not seen it.
Is that utopia?
They say I can join
or might let me in.
Password, what password?
They say there is.
It must exist.
Stupid me, forgetful me;
did utopia leave
with the magician?

Or is it still under—
the broken streetlight?
In the gutter?
Or behind the Cabots' fence?

GOD

He's a funny old squirt.
A real jokester.
He loves to tease and toy.
Disasters are His favorites.
Rather, man-made disasters
. . . to be politically correct.
Oh hell, in keeping
with the theme,
He's a She that loves
screwing with folk's
lives.
Or watching them scream
when bombs get tossed
into ice cream parlors.
But that's not the punchline.
That comes—bada-bing—
when they pray.
How can She
be so mean?
Laughter all around.
'Cuz She runs parallel
with man.
She never touches him.
Or intrudes.
For good or evil.

She never intersects.
Ask any atheist
who can't shake
. . . the bitch . . .
from his peripheral vision.
Now that's funny.
At least it was
in the Sixties
when She saw Herself
on the cover of TIME
magazine.
BEARDED.
Being declared dead
or questioning Her . . .
existence.
When the mere fact
that She . . .
pissed her pants
in the comic disbelief
that men,
like women,
deny what babies know—
the Almighty
merely oversees
the place.

NAMES

What's in a name?
Everything you bastard.
There behind the barn.
Budding breasts,
beer, bullshit and biceps.
Forget the masturbation.
They'll do the darling.
Who?
The men.
No boys.
They'll wait their turn.
Turn?
Of the screw.
Who?
Norma Jeane
you idiot.
That's not
the girl
I know.
She's all
dreamy
with riches
and power
and men so handsome
that boys don't exist.
But sadness dawns.
For whom?

Marilyn
you cretin.
Like changing names—
changes the woman?
Nah, from crib
to cradle
they're always
falling stars . . .
or the girl
back home.

PRYOR

Unlike
his homeboy
. . . Honest Abe . . .
America's most
divisive gangster . . .
King Richard
was the country's
greatest uniter.
Well almost—
but no bananas.
So close,
and yet,
so far.
With
twisted
rednecks
and
sadistic
crackers
becoming
laughing stocks.
While the KKK
was a murderous
stutter.
And Polack jokes
old school.
Unlike the gooks
and slopes

who won a war
. . . to become
the newest
adoptees . . .
and given away
to wops
called Guidos
who'd long been
. . . matinée idols
riding the rails
of a kraut's train
built
by chink-chongs,
coast to coast,
hand-in-hand
with Micks
of the Limey
persuasion
and a wetback's
might,
but like Dick's words
—his slander and slang—
he too was enslaved
by the gallows
humor
of history
where salt
rubbed
the peppered wounds

with an insidious
spice
of
mastery
wrapped
in the litmus paper
of humanity . . .
where certain people
tasted nothing
and others
only the acidity
of burning flesh
or meat hung
for curing.
Meaning that even—
for a King
as astounding
as Richard:
the dish
was too hot
to be cooled
. . . too jive . . .
with soulful chefs
to be emancipated
for such dour
flavors.
When even the hippest
instructions
couldn't bake

the taste
from the offering's
irrelevant moniker
no matter how much
he punch-lined
. . . whipped or fried . . .
the sheer idiocy
. . . if not savagery . . .
of the past recipes
—filed under N—
against
current ingredients.
With the main fix'ins
forever—a Devil's food—
that only certain people
can say or savor
without the discrimination
of tang or time . . .
but only the poison
that empowers
the fiery cross
with an eternal
Angel's dust
of moral starvation
and the endless
hunger
for an equal piece
of a pie

that's so ravenously
consumed
by some,
and equally
regurgitated
by others.

GHOSTS

They're alive . . .
standing behind
the reception desk.
Or wearing the sheets
versus soiling them.
Sunning poolside,
then diving in the dry end;
while drinking
out of glass containers.
Ignoring the rules—
of abandoned,
roadside motels . . .
where most spooks
are housed.
Especially the fly-by night
enterprises.
Located off the interstate.
And by-passed by
the super highways
that don't cotton to phantoms.
Not the younger ones anyway.
Sure they'll steer you towards
the famous places . . .
that *George Washington* haunts.
But that's not Grandma.
Or Uncle Fred.
And it's most definitely not
those teenage parents

. . . on the run.
Stopping
at the Dreamland Motel
to escape
a long dead father-in-law
. . . who wants to strangle
the perpetrator
of the pie . . .
in his daughter's oven.
These are the true ghouls.
Living large—
in their descendants' minds.
They don't shriek or moan
or rattle a chain,
hell, they'd kick their own ass
for banging on the walls.
If they weren't invisible.
No, these apparitions
drip the blood the medic
talked about
and the washerwoman
can't remove . . .
from her essence
—her hands—
or the bathroom floor.
Nothing wipes clean
these goblins.
As they both mercifully,
and without pity,

stain the memory
with spirits
that never die
... and specters
that are still part ...
of the present
whole.

COMPLETE CONCENTRATION

Treblinka
forever lies over my U.S. hills
Where trains do roll
through my childhood still
Day skies darken
and night skies glow
Fertilized grass, green and grows
Over the dead and dying souls
Stuffed headfirst in living holes

All-American Boy Born 19

A skull-white moon shines above
While whore-forced Jew
makes camp-time love
Death is sought as end of whole
Not so
when this bestial train
does roll
across stone bridges
the boxcars slide
Clickity-clack
buries star-crossed sighs

All-American Boy Born 1

Beyond dry creeks my train flies past
Drunken driver blows a final blast

Our Polish vodka kills the pain
Shots drown screams in snow and rain
Trains connect from miles around
To dump their load in my hometown

All-American Boy Born

Childhood recalls trains as fun
Now they warn to forget its run
The train returns,
swift with lightened load
And travels back to the deadman's road
Cars all packed with skintight bone
I don't listen to those alone

All-American Boy Bo

Sidetracked screams waif
about my fears
Fresh smoked flesh
distilled my tears
I've a drunken knowledge
of what I've done
I know it all, yet told no one

All-American Boy

Like the Hitler's mid-wife
in Braunau

40

I knew of horror,
then and now
Rosa Horl delivered
our devil's kin
I knew him well
and let him in

All-American

My heart raved
against that bastard's
"murderous race!"
Yet the Hebrew, a queer, any "ist"
could take my place
Christian screams rang in my ears
But nothing took, nothing near
I knew of torture, yet told no one
Never admit what I had done

All-America

"They," occupied us from within
"We," decreed it
their deadly sin
Our Headmen ordered
and turned their backs
As I laid
the state-run tracks
While
they trooped

41

in lines
towards
well-scrubbed shacks
And freed ash rose
from store bought
stacks

All-Americ

Red embers swirled
in a dull black night
Kike crazed communist
on gypsied flight
Fires raged hotter
and my time grew short
Still I had nothing
to report

All Ame

Cremains flew higher
than I could go
Condemned to silence
for what I know

All A

Their smell
no longer spreads earthbound
Its stench

became my sacred ground
Blood-dried trails
line the path I plod
I dare not touch
the blistered sod
From this soiled earth,
truth could grow
With seeds of hate
from what I know

All

Now
my stifled screams
ring mountain peaks
I lived gagged,
I cannot speak
My tribe once sang
"Fight till our new man comes"
But I fear him
like my father's son

A

For I am that old man
whose mind does reek
I wait silently,
never once I speak.

BLACK FRIDAY

(An Urban Myth)

That's the day the studs
were sold.
Along with girls
of childbearing age.
Purchased to harvest
the crops
after Thanksgiving Day.
But that feasting—
was soon to end . . .
the old and ghastly ways.
In a war so uncivil
that no animal would
engage.
Curtailing the sacred
. . . chivalry . . .
in a sick
and burning rage.
Of souls hung high
upon a cross—
of a coldly collective grave.
Burying deep the dreams
left undead.
To wave the communal flag.
* * *
Thus paging a new
triumvirate
. . . that trumpeted

44

an American We.
Declaring for all mankind
what freedom
was supposed to be.
When the first—
of these three Heralds
delivered a dream
from mountain tops.
Freedom rang.
And children sang
a song
until it stopped.
While another . . .
of the Triad
fought visions
with reveries.
Winning battles
with butterflies—
stinging bees.
And the Third
imagined
a world composed
of only sovereign men.
A faith he embraced.
Late in life.
Exalting it
. . . with his . . .
X
* * *

Thus assigning
his commitment . . .

to the fires of dignity.
Forging man's most sacred traits
—with a steely autonomy.
Embodying his fidelity
within this sovereign state
of Three.
A hero of the heart
that counterfeits
. . . couldn't be.
So, enlightened by collectives
of designed diversity—
impersonators of the past—
dashed in
donning their legacies.

* * *

A frivolity
of such entitlement
it obliterated all self-rule.
Curtailing the Trio's struggles
—at the peak of years, five score—
turning the fight
for independence
into a trudge
by the living dead
who plunder
days gone by
without a significant . . .
prize ahead.

* * *

Bringing an end
to the war for freedom.

And destroying a civility.
Leaving a Republic
—no shot or chance—
at a whiff of
equality.
* * *

This dead-ended
imaginings
. . . of auction blocks
destroyed.
Resurrecting
the squares—where
agents are employed.
To stock and trade
the industry . . .
with bodies soon discharged.
Selling sold identities
to the effigies
living large,
where masters
of the marketplace—
bond with captains
of the arts . . .
standing in solidarity
with those . . .
who play their part;
of bidding high
and buying low.
* * *

Those Creatures
and their comforts.
* * *
Plus the fortunes
of their fame.
Falling in thanksgiving
for their disembodied names.

DANCERS

Would be writers
if they had any brains.
No, they'd rather be mute
as a swan
or daffy as a duck.
Spreading their wings
like some crazed Icarus
trying to defeat gravity.
Even Einstein knew
. . . that was nutzo.
Besides, it's impossible—
to make a buck
doing the improbable.
Or have toes that don't
look like freak shows.
Or granny ankles.
Then there's the body type.
A slice of pie
can blow a career
apart
if they weren't so crazy.
They'd also know a novel
. . . stretching the truth . . .
is far easier than
shredding a knee.
Next, there's the sex—
like mannequins
come alive . . .

49

for every peeper.
Perv.
Tom, Dick and Mary.
To ogle for the price
of admission . . .
without so much as a
criminal charge.
No, if dancers
weren't dummies
they'd know that . . .
penning love stories
—in thin air—
is a fool's gold.

TRANSGENDER

Because of gravity
—the attraction of—
—two bodies—
towards the other
... I crash landed.
On this planet.
Yet knew I'd have to
... rocket away again.
At least that's what
the instruments said.
I honestly hoped,
like family at home,
this too was my ...
docking station.
But something misfired.
Setting the obvious
—or not—
of this celestial mission
ablaze.
Reigniting the candle
to my spaceship.
Sending me speeding
towards the heavens
for another ride.
Alone.

At warp speed.
Splitting time
and space
in two.
Reassigning the stars
into birth lights.
Birthright?
Not yet.
For the delivery
of a safe return
means . . . remolding
the egg of time
with a cell of space.
Reproducing
the original me.
Ending this trip
of an out'a
—body experience—
with a reclaiming
of this world
called earth.
In my true
and rightful name.

SKIRTS

Are the hems
of heaven
in a man's eyes.
With calves
hooking
like ladders
to muscled thighs
... displacing
Rapunzel's hair
with dreams
... if not ...
needs and wishes.
Leading,
not to a window
of escape,
but gates beyond ...
his imaginings.
Afresh.
Transformed.
Revisiting
—the impossible—
remembrances
of a childhood
embrace
or kiss
of innocence.
The unrealized.

The forgotten, the found
or purposely destroyed.
Reconnecting
the transcendent mix
of manhood
with the boy . . .
while the private
realms
of ladyship
—above waist high—
precede
his jurisdictions
of influence
or possession
. . . in this world
of make-believe.

LEFT VERSUS RIGHT

Lefties
have decreed
there's no immorality
in lying.
Nothing
that can't be
explained away.
And God forbid
it's not a sin.
Like there's no
bad karma
or true evil.
That . . .
inhumanity
is for haters
believing
might
is
right.

HELLFIRES SHAKE THE BLUES

Nothing kills time
Better than an autopsy of war
Since the first conflict
We've prided ourselves
On dissection and documentation
The baptisms of fire
As all civil battles
Begin with handsome warriors
Proud and brave
We hiss at the rise of villains
Cheer our side
And reverently convince ourselves
We've done good for God
Using our wrath
God's wrath
Our direction
God's direction
As our path
Destruction is a decree
Of the highest order
But as times change
So do commands and objectives
From pious conquest
To holy survival
As warrior's skin shrinks taut
Over cheekbones
And sloppy loose

56

Around mouth and eyes
Lips no longer form . . .
in warm kisses
Of love
But hiss . . .
the frozen commands
Of rape
As killers'
And victims' eyes
Blink with incredulity
At the hallowed madness
Yet they play the part
The role
With the disguised righteousness
Of sacrifice
And only in this . . .
combative state
Of opposites
This inhumed mentality
Can one continue to fight
And die
Via extermination
Of thought
And rationality
Can one carry the banner
The martyr's step
That zealots
Love to rehash
Through the bravery

Of the dead
Crushing
The perpetrators
Of The Cause
By celebrating
The recreation
of battles
With bombs bursting
in air, land, and sea
"Ooohhhhs" and "aahhhhhs"
As children memorialize
One's savagery
By demolishing
The beast
Within the callousness
Of it all
This parading
Band playing, flag waving
Twirlerettes trooping
Is the dreamlike state
That spews
A puce colored cusp
Of smoke and mirrors
Where proper murderers
And fashionable killers
Grasp the imagination
Creating a physicalness
Of brutality
Where one can feel

And weep
In the most sensual
Untouched regions
Of the heart
Allowing wise men
To teach the wisdom
Of going over the top
To witness
and stand erect
Obeying the bugle's call
Inhaling the deadly incense
Of gunpowder
Charged
With rolls of thunder
Exploding
To watch the enemy
Flail and fall
Failing to escape
Upon the movie screen
Minus the stench
Or flies
Filming the decay
Heightening the carnage
While one turns
Towards another's aim
Testing his goodness
Vindicating his position
Justifying the justifications
—their chosenness—
of God

As the sniper mis-fires
Saving the crusade
With a militaristic
Underworld
Where hellfires
Shake the blues
Leaving war
And hate
As the final comfort
The solo source
of human confirmation
The last true . . .
intercourse
Or final thrust
Between man
Searing the death rattles
Of battles
And the hard won magic
Of existence
With a last
. . . furious blast . . .
of triumphant sound.

O SHEPHERD, OUR SHEPHERD

Hopelessly lost
in the pastures
of war.
Our weary woes
. . . raged aloft . . .
protesting the insanity
of endless battles
against the wolves
who came
to devour
and destroy
in the name
of their Godless God.
Who rained blood
from the heavens.
Turning the grass
to meat red
and our hearts
to the colorlessness
of unhealable wounds.
When O Shepherd
Our Shepherd
your essence
flowered
from war-scarred
battlefields

of ignorance and bliss.
And rose like a drover
of peace and harmony . . .
before our flock
of humanism and love.
Spiritually
turning us
from sheep
—for some oppressive tenet—
to physical manifestations
of the heroic.
All shapes and forms . . .
agelessly cloaked
in the righteousness
of history . . .
O Shepherd
Our Shepherd
As the crook
of your oneness
united—
our rudderless herd.
We now follow your lead
and march, not like lambs
to slaughter,
but as kith and kin

through your meadows
of peace and justice.
Keeping both the wolves
... and their unholiness ...
at bay—
with rockets rife with stone
and explosions of adoration.
Without a single blast
of protest
or objection
that detonated
the idolatry
of madness and greed
from our blackest
past.

CRIMINALITY

Oh the preciousness
of being misunderstood.
It gives such time
and space
to filch their innocence
and unwillingness
to believe
that my endeavors
. . . hopes and dreams . . .
are as gleefully
unobtainable
as their true love
of houses
with white picket fences
and fresh faced babes
that bathe naked
in the cleansing
sinks of normality.
Where the unthinkable
burns beneath
the surface
of visions like me—
as a friend or neighbor
who blisters their imaginings
with the wanton,
inconceivability,

that our joy
and happiness
. . . like family . . .
boils in the same pot.
And no amount
. . . of cold water . . .
tossed in the face
of reality
can make me value
their understanding
of life.
Any more than they
can wash their hands
of the roiling delight
I receive
from continuously abusing
their sympathies.

STRIPPER

An empress
. . . Nubian black . . .
emerged on stage.
The music beat.
The dance pounded.
Without warning,
like a bird of prey,
she stood stock still.
Hovering . . .
over the sexual quagmire.
Studying it.
Deciding on the kill.
Before slowly voguing
down a raised runway . . .
running parallel to the bar.
All lit like a landing strip
for celestial spaceships.
Glowing a neon blue.
Luminously smudging
her skin
with oily shadows
of light and dark.
Heightening the anticipation
. . . the insanity . . .
of her getup.
Leather chaps, vest, and a Stetson—
pink as sex itself.

And strapped,
like a garrot
—to a highly burnished
thigh—
was a holstered weapon
. . . so dangerously long
its threats were multiple.
Like her visage—
that exuded
an impertinence
past royalty.
One that knew only
the satisfaction
of her own hand:
that snatched
her vest open and shut . . .
exposing monstrous breasts
that wavered and crested
like hunchbacked serpents
roiling above a waist
as round as a man's hands
. . . strangling a lover.
Her fingers
—languished—
within inches of a G-string.
A rawhide patch
covered the wonder below.
Then, striking quick as a rattler
she drew the six-shooter,

firing a blank into space.
The shot was loud
but nobody flinched.
Not a sound
from the unseen faces;
while smoke drooled
from the weapon's snout.
The air went dead—
as she stripped bare,
except, for her sidearm.
She stood cowgirl proud.
Exposed.
Before lowering herself
in a constipated squat,
grimacing, she took aim
on the invisible mugs
that spectated cold and hard.
The music stopped.
A shootout.
Five shots blazed
into the blackness.
Nothing.
Not a sound.
Silence.
Standing upright,
with nothing else to bare,
she threw her head
straight back . . .
and wantonly slid

the red-hot barrel
deep down her throat.
Engorging it.
A manlike
Adam's Apple appeared.
It bulged and bounced.
Click.
Click, click, click.
A glass tipped.
A beer bottle tumbled.
A new song throbbed.
A flat chested Caucasian
. . . took her place.

TATS

Beauty behold
for it is me!
A flash of nirvana!
Spoken
in the glossiest
of psalms
and languages unknown.
All Buddhist.
And Sanskrit.
Speaking of the dead.
Resurrected.
On my canvas!
I carry their essence
within fists . . .
full of skin and bones.
And hearts.
Spliced with knives.
Bleeding me
into a masterwork!
A tour de force!
Dyed
in another's hand
I wear
the library of my life
skin tight
like a leotard
or third degree burn . . .

that warmly
encompasses mothers
in arms
. . . geometrically . . .
designed as children
chasing
pots of gold
slung low
across my shoulders
and down
my designer chest.
My magnum opus!
As told . . .
through unicorns
and the bumbling
of bees
that sport
insignias
of warriors and braves.
Sending signals
of sexuality
beyond
a flex of muscle.
Head to toe.
Creating me!

As a work of art
. . . a masterpiece . . .
for my age.
All fury
sans the sounds
of genius
. . . severing their ear.
Or penetrating the soul
with bullets of suicide
. . . leaden with paint.
And the madness
of starry nights
and irises
nailed
to museum walls.

DWEEBS

There ain't no app
for alcohol.
Or mind-altering
drugs
for that matter.
There ain't no app
for getting off
'cept porn.
Even then
you got to get
involved
with more
than fingertips
if you're a man—
anyhow.
And not a . . .
cartoon character.
Or a sexless
avatar.
No there ain't no app
for what sears
physicalness
to the heat
of passion.
There ain't no app
for the groans
of pleasure

echoing
in your head.
There ain't no app
for the reverberations
of whispers
past.
Or being alone
in bed
. . . when . . .
the wake-up call
is the warmest
reassurance
of romance
and devotion.
No,
that there ain't no app
for a coffee high
or the heartfelt scents
of eggs and bacon
. . . being fried
by last night's love.

POLLOCK

There's a language
nobody speaks.
When coming of age.
Or slightly younger.
For a kid
in shit-kicker boots
donning butch cuts
as the apple
of a mother's eye.
Or a beloved
son
nobody wanted.
Even a snitch witch
. . . a poor little miss . . .
singing in circles.
They
all know a language
nobody speaks.
Screaming fearfully.
Or whispering altruistically.
This muteness
that sensitive
children know—
as a terrible rumble
tucked away inside
. . . like a ticking
time bomb

unarticulated,
suffocating,
until that day . . .
the first day
of field-tripping
to a museum
of past modernity
and the present Now.
Where canvased skies
—oiled in the voices
of rainbows—
and alternative lives
. . . burst open.
And sentience
rains out.
Speaking
the unspoken
in artistic tongues
. . . untied . . .
with the soundlessness
of words painted
deep within
the blossom
of a maturing
child's mind.

ED

Fuck yes,
I respect you.
Ok Ok.
I love you.
Sure that too.
Ooooh baby!
Ooooh girl!
Damn that's good!
Such sweetness.
You're the best.
No No,
I promise I won't.
I won't.
I promise.
Am I good?
JeeeeesUs!
Praise be.
Opps!
I'm sorry.
It won't happen again.
Can't, busy Friday.
But Monday.
It's a date . . .
or a dream . . .
bordering
on a nightmare
of what was once.

A live hand grenade
is now a booby trap
that doesn't go off,
explode.
Even with voodoo . . .
there's a timer now
. . . if you're lucky.
But no tripwire.
No hair trigger.
And definitely
not a flip switch.
Man's most powerful
armament
is relegated
to a peashooter
that fires aimlessly
like shots
in the dark.
But not to worry.
No complaints.
The body count's
been taken
and the tolls
are in . . .
like a practical joke.
Or an external dementia—
what was once cocked
and loaded

with the safety
perpetually off . . .
is now a retired
gunslinger
out of Tombstone.
Sentenced.
Under lock
and key.
While harmlessly
jailed away.

RESPECT

Why kill him?
He didn't know you . . .
from Adam.
Riders sat stunned.
Trapped.
Screams rang out.
The bus stopped.
They exited
along with . . .
everybody else;
except the stranger.
The stiff.
Why cap him?
He didn't know you . . .
from Adam.
He should have.
He'd never —
seen you before.
He'd seen me now
. . . he looked me . . .
straight in the eyes.
What's that supposed
to mean?
He owed me.
What?
To go deaf—
dumb and blind.
But he didn't know you
. . .from Adam.
He does now.

IT'S All SCAT

Them black cats
Crossing the bar
With rats watchin'
Their slave green eyes
Bouncing over dance floors
As ghosts sit pissed
Sharpening their claws
Waiting to pounce
When the feline chooses
And all hell breaks loose.

REVOLUTIONARIES

Revolution is an erection.
Or at the very least
a long drawn out
orgasm.
With activism
an alcoholic shot
of intellectualism . . .
mixed with a hint of murder.
Or killing.
Or the very least
a wisp
of being a very bad
child.
Driving Daddy nuts
and Mommy
back to the bottle
for the crime
of not having seen,
not recognizing,
not singing
praise be
to the preciousness
of their distraught . . .
sprout.
And for this sin
of omission

all parents
must pay
for their neglect
and ignorance.
Regardless of intent.
Or reason.
Not even self-preservation
can protect them
from this new love
. . . that knows . . .
only the dogma
as the commitment.
With vows of chastity,
meaning,
only the purification
of the unchaste
—at all cost—
without hesitation
or pity.
Turning lovers
into traitors
and friends
into fiends.
While the masturbatory
truth
of self-aggrandizement
becomes gospel
to the only ones
who count.

RACISM

Niggardly thoughts
how can there be?
When slaves—
are the essential
Americans!
And the yammering
class
cast stones
against glass houses
of righteous
indignation.
Where ivory leagues
feel the painful
angst
of dumbass
chicks
and trailer trash
that pump
their bootay
over ching-chang
men
who crash
the books
instead of cooking
them.
Like Indians
with dots

84

and feathers
or past imperialists
who colluded
with Vikings
to blissfully
rape and pillage
the sons
plus daughters
of their mothers'. . .
and fathers' land.
While taking joy
. . . in not standing . . .
on the shoulders
of giants
but hanging them
high.

BIBLE THUMPERS

Christ no, they ain't the toothless
bastards anymore.
Not even the peroxide
shit for brains
or the golfers
in lime green pants
. . . and white . . .
patent leather belts.
Hell no—and praise be—
the newest evangelicals
loathe haters
and gun toters;
along with blue-eyed
cheerleaders
making their bible thick
with the arts
of abs
and women's issues,
plus, puppies dressed
as men
who rationalize
human nature
with words
recalibrated.
Making sin
impossible
and lies

mere misunderstandings
that can be explained
away
in waves of varietals
served at
the highest mass
of diversification
and love
. . . where the faithful . . .
to past convictions
are sweetly
crucified
for doubting
the Gods
on earth.

INK

When he humps
his love
doggystyle
he sees God.
But only if
the lights are on.
Then there's
the missionary
position
and, not so much
. . . but oh'boy . . .
cunnilingus
that's where
parrots and paradise
fly
—at eye level—
just below
the belt line.
And up
. . . while suckling
titties . . .
all forms
of work heave
and ho
with artistic fervor.
From comic
to sublime.

But nothing
as masculine
or cliché
as his
barbwire.
Or Chinese
proverbs.
But that's all
ching-chong
to him.
Spinning his
mind's eye
back to the nips
where Elvis
makes an appearance
. . . along with rose
buds
that trick
his lips
at times.
But heck,
she gets
the killer view
when biting
his neck
and sucking
sweet swastikas in.
Yet, fear not
this is adoration.

Especially
. . . when she licks . . .
the teardrop
dripping down
his cheek . . .
pooling on
a chest
That's Born
To lose.

RAPE

It's so fucking one-sided.
Seriously,
the selfishness
of it all.
Must come
from the confusion
of Neanderthals.
Or before the crack
of dawn.
Back when hair
wasn't wasted
on the sensitive bits,
but worn
like a coat
you couldn't take off
. . . no matter . . .
how hot or cold
the climate change.
But that's no explanation
for the sense
of entitlement
that certain body parts
have for others.
So maybe it wasn't
the ape-men
or monkeys—

it could
have been the dogs
surrounding the camps.
Begging for bones.
But nothing justifies
how or why
evolution
kept the nastiness intact.
It's not like webbed toes
or vestigial muscles.
It's just the dirtiest feat
minus the babies.
Or intended brats.
But that's as demented
as equating it
with adoration . . .
even if the bastard act
has some similarities
with love—
but oh no
. . . oh shit . . .
stop!
Not those opposites
—that teach—
those teachable moments . . .
with pain highlighting pleasure.
Black against white.
Us versus them.
Yes or no?

Is that the reason
we seek
this apish savagery?
This human insult?
This sexual battering?
This naked truth?
Is it truly
nature's way
of both promoting
and safeguarding
the taste
for affection
trumping
the thirst
for brutality?

INTELLECTUALS

Shit for brains
is not the human mind.
It's a light bulb.
Forty watts.
It dims and sparks.
It's powered by
God-knows-what.
The psyche?
The soul?
The MILF
. . . down the street?
Or her muscle-headed
. . . husband . . .
regardless, the ganglion
can't think.
It believes!
Because believing
doesn't drain
the wattage
or strain the system.
True thinking
—outside the church—
—beyond the gospel—
makes foreheads furrow
and temples pound.
No, the correct answers

. . . the appropriate retort . . .
comes from the selfsame
psyche
that eventually
got you laid.
Or plays well
in your current
—circle jerk—
or app society.
That's it!
That's what keeps you
from being called
shit-for-brains.
It's reading
from the exact same bible
as insipid atheist
or evangelical Leftist
and body builders
of any color.
Whatever the group . . .
that you're deliriously
trying to fuck
or get fucked
by.

CONGA LINE

Oh dear God—
not that venomous music.
That pounding beat.
The heat wedded
with youthful sweat.
The inescapable room
packed skin-tight
with smiles most devious
and the sickest grins.
Twinkling eyes.
Ancient lips.
Ageless cleavages,
bounce and heave . . .
locking sightlines
to nooks
and crannies
that've come and passed
. . . only to come again;
while boozy hoots
rise and quake
and shimmying people
hideously band together
—not in a common mind—
but a single body.
Devilishly snaking
around the room.
Sweet Jesus . . .

are Aunt Margo's boobies
leading the way
. . . and Father Frank's
butt . . . the beginning
and end of this joke
"That if one doesn't succumb,"
to becoming
part of the serpent
—that the familial nature
of the dance—
will crush him
with contractions.

ANTI-WAR

I'm a ghost
crying out . . .
from plantations
and Auschwitz
plus,
hellholes before
and since.
Come save us.
We beg you.
Come save us.
It falls
upon deaf ears
against violence
done unto us
. . . by them.
Those who know
no violence
done unto them
. . . seeing God's
work . . .
in their
eyes
as Lord
and Savior
by leaving us
here to die.

CLIMAX

Hey girl
I got one too.
What?
A button.
Not a G-Spot?
No, it's bigger than that.
So when'ja get it?
What?
Your so-called button.
Always had it,
but it didn't work at first.
Didn't work at all?
Not completely.
When then?
At the age of confusion.
Not consent?
Utter confusion . . .
didn't know good
from bad.
Me too.
Except I knew
which hand to use.
It's not always . . .
done that way.
Which way?
Alone.
Two can turn it on.

Or push the button.
Is it red?
Is what red?
The button.
Like the one pushed
. . . to launch . . .
warheads?
In my case, yes.
So it's a weapon?
Sometimes.
Of mass destruction?
Depends who's on . . .
the other end.
The receiving end, you mean?
I only know what I mean
—before it explodes—
after, everything's a crapshoot.
There's no options?
Like what?
A nuclear option,
I suppose.
You suppose what?
There's always
a love
to bomb.

PORN

There's a step missing.
Gone.
There's money
and an interesting filth.
But there's no front,
nor back, only a middle.
If done straight-up.
There's either deadness
or a wicked hate.
Drugged—
it's nearly a party
. . . minus the balloons . . .
or floppy footed clowns.
Noses might be red
and violets are always blue,
but the sweat and the groan
isn't you.
It's for a face in the gloom.
A spirit so lost
it'd make a mother weep
—with bones and skin—
mixed in a blender
and poured into a mold.
Sometimes recognizable,
but mostly not.

Except if you're a man.
A hard-on can't be faked.
Aggression is aggression.
The vital ingredient.
A loveless truth
with dominance a staple.
Sympathy, unbeknownst.
But it's all misplaced
and ends
before anything ever begins—
and a life is formed.

A JUNKYARD DOG

Knows no love.
Gives no love.
But hobbles heroically
to save the day . . .
against thieves
and hooligans
that cut the fence . . .
stealing the master's keys
. . . unlocking the safe;
while fisting a gun—
like a sword of mightiness.
Ending the attack.
In one shot.
Suffering only torn pants.
While a yelp echoes
into the abyss
of loyalty.

THE CIRCUS

I hate
waking in this alley.
Where crack-shits
flow
like chocolate sauce.
At least I'm not
a constipated
ass-wipe
like that Suit
in the crosswalk.
Look at the poor bastard.
Probably escapes
Pleasantville
every morning
like his tits
are on fire
leaving the brat—
bastards behind
to burn
and his wife
time to think
about new ways
of getting laid.
Shit, I'd smile
at his fucking dilemma
if I only had teeth.

It's one
of the downsides
of crank—
besides believing
you got a crystal ball
that sees a pathetic prick's
life . . .
looking down
on scumbags
like me.
Probably deluding himself
with the thought
that I screw crack whores
for rock
and a blow job
. . . that he don't get . . .
no'moe.
Plus, how the progressive
. . . pansy-asses . . .
give me a hand,
a hand-up
—like the hand job—
he's forced to give himself.
While I'm thinking
the sad bastard's
even gott'a pay
his own medical bills.
Shit man . . . I just OD

and whoopee-doo
I'm scraped
from these urine
. . . soaked streets . . .
to lie pretty
as I please
on clean sheets—
with the city
paying the freight.
Unless, of course,
one of them lazy wetbacks
is hoggin' the space.
Should'a'shot'em
at the border . . .
as they don't know shit
. . . about how we
run this place.
Or the rat race
that ol' Suits . . .
and I
live our lives
by.

RATS

Oh, beloved.
Sweet vermin.
Your cupidity
for rot and waste
. . . humans hold so dear.
Through man's acceptance
and a feminine need
to achieve the grace
of a purposeful life
. . . is found . . .
within your multitudinous
gifts
of sickness and disease.
For nowhere else
can one rise
so high
above the natural core
as with your acquaintance
—dearest friend—
not even the mighty
cockroach
can hold a candle
to your infectious Self.
All your being,
all your worth,
justifies
the opposite
of your equal.

107

Love!
Love . . .
is dependent on you.
For survival.
As hate
. . . a hate . . .
a single disgust
within All for you—
makes you the poster boy
for duteous instances
and understanding
. . . if not justification . . .
of why love holding hands
with loathing
is a righteous
annihilation.
This is an inheritance
. . . from birth:
serving in equal times
with the killing fields
and loving thy neighbor.
Like your eradication
being the heartwarming,
if not soul saving,
objectification
of the most honorable
extermination—
in the name
of love.

TASTELESS

My first billion
was conceived
in my mother's basement.
The one with the unused
rec-room
and fold-out bed.
Not in the light
of day . . .
for the casement
windows
were covered
with spunk
stained sheets
. . . products . . .
of computer porn
when I wasn't decoding
my code.
The world's code.
But definitely not
the da Vinci code.
Whoever that idiot
bastard is, or was,
like painting some bitch
—with a shit-eating grin—
is priceless?

A bimbo who
wouldn't know
an app
from my a-hole . . .
isn't of any worth
. . . or earthly value.
Hell,
Beavers and Buttheads
are more the pussy
. . . the hairy womb . . .
for birthing
my next project.
Way better
than any so-called artist
. . . or the uselessness . . .
they call art.
It's all as worthless
and unproductive
as communicating
with some perfunctory
—dipwads—
when there's no IPO
to offer.

ILLEGAL

I'm going home.
I belong there.
I deserve that place.
I've never seen
a hill
nor dale
or smelled
a wisp of spring.
I'm going home now.
I belong there.
I deserve that place.
I've never seen
a waterslide
nor swimming pool
or baked
in a summer sun.
I'm going home, soon.
I belong there.
I deserve that place.
I've never seen
a leaf turn
nor heard
the thunder storm.
I'm going home—

in future times.
I belong there.
I deserve that place.
I've never seen
a snowfall
nor felt
the ice break
. . . except . . .
here,
today.

SEX

The answer
is always on the tip
of my tongue . . .
or hopefully
theirs.
But everything changes
once respect
crawls
into bed . . .
as a threesome.
It's no animal.
More like a flower.
A rose . . .
without the bleeding.
Because the creature
no longer bites,
rips or tears,
leaving the lick
as the thrust
while praying
that love
is the orgasm
and sex
the seed.

SUCKER PUNCHED

Exiting the birth canal
I was confronted
by a murder
of liars.
All complicit in their
self-preservation.
Living thoughts
like truths.
Speaking words
to the flock
as if gospel
. . . while spewing . . .
sunshine smiles
of deception
and pathology.
This was my world.
This was family.
Friends and neighbors.
This was my starting point
for the sprint
towards an end
of this blank
and confusing
spin zone.
Where my lie
was the self-serving
belief
in their veracity

114

and need to condone—
their saintliness
by putting myself down.
To lose.
Becoming lesser
than their ignorance.
Grinning the grin
of conspiracy
unable to believe,
to grasp,
their treachery . . .
towards the world
at large—
was nothing more
than my wickedness.
My inability
to abide
by the common good.
To take their verbal
deceits
up the ass
and swallow them whole.
To become
my own impregnator,
incestuously infecting
my unborn egg
with their mutant
spunk and jive.

Obediently . . .
producing their twin.
Repopulating the plantation
as a good girl
in my att'a boy
disguise.

KINDNESS

It's the most brutal
of bombshells.
An improvised
explosive . . .
that can kill
if terrorists
get their hands
on it—
manipulating it
for their own
purposes.
Using it
to detonate
against its source,
because the explosion
of true benevolence
is more powerful
than love
as it fires
past the self
. . . beyond . . .
all known entities—
towards strongholds
of the darkest
pathology

that is only breeched
—exposed—
and routed
from the shadows
with the kindest
of light.

LOVER AS DAWN CAT

Low fog crept over our rise tonight
Seeped and dipped in hunchbacked sight
Till streetlight webbed our low-gear hill
And dawn crouched on window sill

A tail tipped thought through fine air mist
Hissing aloft her delicate kiss
We crossed slick streets in shades of night,
no rush, no wrong or right

Soft shadow brought we two to edge
Then jumped upon the wooden ledge
Tightwired, cat skipped a dance
Soft tapped paws stepped high in prance

Longhaired lover stroked the fur
Pulled it tight, a single purr
Lover's hand stretched upon the face
Stiffer the tail rose in space

Higher and higher the head did pose
Till nothing existed 'cept tail and nose
Her final rub in search of chest
Brought a bite, a nip, teeth scraped flesh.

SELFIE!

Selfie, selfie!
Is that me?
Its eye
looks different
than mine.
Its body is hard
and cold.
Its memory
OMG!
It's humongous
wheeee!
I'm sending myself
spinning
around the world
where guys
get off
and gals too.
Shoot another
naked in the bathroom
. . . gaming the mirror.
But is that me?
Really!
Is that me?
Shoot another!

Can't they see?
Can't I?
I'm shooting myself
. . . with my own hand
I'm coming into focus—
like masturbation.
Shoot, shoot, shoot!
With my own hand . . .
I'm coming into focus
. . . but is that me?

CELEBRITY

Look at me!
Look at me!
Stop!
And look at me!
I'm sexier
than your dreams.
I'm more than you
could ever hope for.
I'm a sun.
A moon.
A star on earth.
I'm all yours
and yours alone . . .
making your existence
mine—
and mine to own.
But I can't taste—
the world anymore.
They've taken that away
. . . from me.
You've taken that away
. . . from me.
Whoever asked you
to look
my way.

SHOES

Men know nothing
of shoes.
Sure shoes stop
broken glass
from lancing
corns.
And screw wingtips.
Boring as dog shit.
Attraction's . . .
the name of the game
for both honeys
and dons.
With athlete's feet
giving work
. . . the boot.
Or hushes
the puppies.
But women
know no economy
—and forget practicality—
when it comes
to footwear.
No highs or lows.
It's an unspoken
truth.

A need.
A magic
—no man—
can heed . . .
only diminish.
If not desecrate.
For a woman's foot
is the connecting
rod
thrust deep
into mother Earth;
linking the lady
to all below.
Surfacing
and floating . . . above . . .
slipping shoes
into a solo dance
—designed for two—
or none
at all.

NATURAL CAUSES

Life's
a chump's game.
It's all planned—
obsolescence.
With baby wrinkles
turning
. . . into troughs
of mockery
and body hair
making fools
of us all . . .
marauding about
in matching outfits
with original
. . . hair color . . .
before turning
silver
or blanching
Death White
like fibrous fiends
predatorily
using our bodies
like time charts
for expiring warranties

. . . as they first . . .
lurk about confused
and embarrassed
by themselves
and their sheer
existence.
Before boldly arising
from the private
parts
—like sexual
psychopaths—
deviously penetrating
nose and ears
. . . too slothful . . .
to scale
the interior
and seed
the summit
with living follicles.
Leaving—
only denuded skin,
like baby butts,
atop old Farts'
heads.
Before turning
their attention
to the most sensual . . .
lips and chins . . .

thrusting themselves out
. . . like war pikes
against a kiss
from those
now wearing
pelt coats
on the warmest
days.
With bear shag
sprouting from
shoulders
to chests
. . . once as smooth . . .
. . . and caressable . . .
as the marble
marker
being foisted
upon one's grave.

BUKOWSKI

That shitfaced
pig!
Nah, macho man.
Loving
the limbs
of ladies
or the fattest
asses
with smallish
breast
and suckable
nips . . .
like the quim-colored lips
of dead
soldiers.
Where beer
once flowed
in winy utterances
. . . mixing sex
with fucking,
then love.
Or appreciation
of mirrors . . .
healing acne
with wisdom
or cocktails
that pussy foot

128

from sacks
to racetracks
and back.
To paddocks . . .
of saddles
and whips
plus horns
and leads . . .
with harnesses
that mount
and cinch
the saddlebags
in stirrups
of lust
. . . as fleshy bits
rope heartache
to the rhyming
of losers
and winners
who're eternally
trumped
for never
having placed
the bet
—that women who blush—
train their flanks
to lap
the track

where mares
and stallions
collide
in a world
of wonder
and words
wasted
unless the final
thrust
is
human nature
and
human nature
is
the last word
of his story.

DEATH

You fear death?
I know him intimately.
Hell, I give the bastard
. . . sugar.
He lives two doors
down.
I also threaten him
for playing
his music
too loud.
And he tells me—
to go to hell.
But that's not my beef.
He raps on my door
then runs away.
Scaring the shit
out'a me.
But not the little ones.
The babies.
They don't give . . .
a rat's ass about him.
What'ya afraid of
they mock.
He's only a ghost,
for heaven's sake.

So I shiver
as I repeatedly
deny him
. . . screaming . . .
he's got the wrong
—fucking address!

A FANTASY

Baby . . .
way back when . . .
it was
another world.
A parallel dream.
The sunshine.
Over rainbows.
And under seas
of green,
Or a big
fucking car.
With dangling
dingo balls.
And ladyfingers
to eat.
On cream colored
seats
spread
like silken sheets.
Then snap,
crackle, and pop
. . . it's quicksilver
slipping through
the fingers . . .
draining away
and backing-up.
Splashing old jokes

. . . in black ankle socks . . .
against super sexing,
black, net stockings.
Spewing forth
the sludge
of lust lost.
And love
forgotten.
As the wrist
falls asleep
and the groans,
unsatisfied.

AN INTERIOR EXPOSED

Youth never sees out.
It's all in here.
Waiting for a coronation.
To rise supreme.
No one knows me.
But I know all.
Nothing is.
Nothing will.
I hold existence in my palm.
But the day darkens
. . . or passes . . .
the body writhes and splits.
Orgasms twitch on by.
Leaving me holding the bag.
With hands as useless as the past.
Breathing breaths unknown.
Past honesty and truth
confused
by synapsis stuttering.
This is the sunrise
and set.
That senses a remembrance—
of a life once conjured:
as mine.
To own.

CONTACTS

When did my
address book
turn into a
graveyard?
Cell phones.
E-mail.
It once consisted
of living things,
but as the years
. . . slid by . . .
the ringtones
dimmed
and the mail
went undelivered.
Unreturned.
Unanswered.
Where things
once hummed . . .
crickets
now rule . . .
the silence.
Like a
—dead letter file—
masked in memories
and meaningless
names.

ARE YOU

. . . the right size
for me?
The right shape?
No size.
Too big?
Or too small?
Growing?
Shrinking?
Are you . . .
the right size
for me?

ARTIST

Suicide
becomes the inevitable
stroke of life.
The scream—
is the first.
Well, not so much
a scream . . .
as a belief.

BARTENDERS

The good ones,
damn!
They got crazy little fish eyes.
Handsome.
Fucking beautiful.
As dopey as your first dog.
Don't forget the thugs,
the snakes,
the honest and true.
They're reeling you in.
Not really.
But they're reeling you in.
They don't even want you there
. . . in a way . . .
I mean, you're disrupting
their understanding
of themselves
—and potential fucks—
or former lays.
But God Almighty
. . . and shit on a log . . .
they gott'a make rent too.
So back to you.
Back to them.
Back to the buzz
that lives
and dies.
Back to the community,
"Long live the Queen!"
"The King is dead!"

139

NARCO NOMADS

Your swagger
and fearsome smile
—through still virgin teeth—
are a badge of honor
against your rape,
molestation,
creature comforts
. . . Baddy Daddies . . .
of a home long left.
Fostering your belief,
or subtle intuition,
that you can beat
the odds
of this idiot's joke
as told by children
a million different ways
with the hoariest
of punchlines—
remaining the same . . .
you're crap on stilts
when walking the streets.
There's no net
of protection
or safety
and your pit bull
is toothless in defense.

He's only a portend
of an animal like
existence.
Where love
is a doggy-hump
of any warm appendage,
dead or alive.
And caring,
and brotherhood,
comes from the sister
with the next fix.
It's no black
or white thing . . .
it's just that home
ain't never coming back.

AGE

What the fuck!
When'd that pockmarked
bastard appear?
Jesus Christ . . .
I laughed
at it.
Nah, nah.
Na-nah-na.
You can't catch
me.
Never.
Ever.
Only sick shits
catch your disease.
Like street scum.
Sewer rats.
Social pimps.
Preppie freaks . . .
and moneyed
tards from Mars.
No, not me.
So what's with . . .
my body slowing.
Time speeds.
Thoughts mock
my invincibility

and wave
at Death—
like a pal.
Or distant . . .
relative.
He ain't so bad
. . . once you get . . .
to know Him.
Or accept Him
in the house.
Holy shit!
No, really
—who the fuck—
let that prick in?
Nature?
Why you rat—
bastard . . .
mother fuck!
No, I didn't hear
or see You
coming.
But now
You're
here . . .
give my best
to yesterday.

CATLIKE

You're in the curl.
The wave's break.
Arms embracing knees.
Chin tucked in.
Nakedly surfing
towards . . .
a distant shore.
When the surge
. . . sleeps . . .
suspending animation
. . . placing the world
on hold.
Preparing . . .
to take the blow.
Or rush.
By seizing the surf—
pulling the foam
white sheet
up.
Suffocating.
Tumbling facelessly
toward a beach
of a long abandoned
terrain.

WHORES

They're hopelessly
living the American
Dream.
Young
and lustful.
Struttin'
their stuff.
With sex
to die for.
In Hollywood scenes
and bedroom communities.
Piling drugs
on high
. . . of mothers . . .
. . . that simper . . .
for their daughters'
surprise.
And daddies
not showing
the back of their hands
but stroke
the hair
of the promised
land.

FASHION

It's all scoop necks
and cleavage.
With long legs
leading
to parts
undisclosed.
It's money honey.
It ain't the clothes.

CUT AND FELLED

A family treed.
Roots and rising
producing drupes
and leaves.
Swinging.
Swaying.
Exposed to the sun
. . . it rains
—winter storms—
while surviving on
the fruits
of its own loins
. . . that fall away
as sustenance
or rotten
to the core.
Complaining that
branches
plus stems
infested them
with worms
as Mother Nature—
sickened by their peals
that seek self-pity—
or worse
. . . understanding . . .

while rolling further
from the tree
that is
. . . all of their . . .
own making.

LOVE

Is a kitty
that don't talk
back.
But meows
and purrs
with every rub
and stroke
. . . coming squarely . . .
in the middle
of the lap.
It nests
with sighs
not scratches.
Warming the cockles
of another's parts.
Draining
the lifeblood
of simps
who know
—only the thrust—
as love
and never
the parry,
or any beauty,
within the beast.

SUICIDE

Is infanticide
if parents
still exist.
Or depending
—on one's—
marital status
. . . or sex . . .
the offing could be
uxoricide
crossed
by a matricide.
And if the corpse
ain't an only . . .
child
toss in
a sororicide
. . . trumped by a
fratricide
but never a
deicide . . .
unless the carcass
was a Marxist
intellect.
Yet,
the horror,
no, the terror

of this taking
—whatever the being
or position
in life—
is easy
as pie.
The choice,
I mean.
When the day comes,
you choose
. . . the noose . . .
or to go out
for a slice
of pizza.

ERRORLESS

I lived life perfectly.
Beyond reproach.
Never a hair out of place.
Rife with gold stars.
Flawless . . .
was my instruction taking.
Paying every due.
With groans coming naturally;
yet more infrequently,
but not the sucking
to the bitter end.
When I failed
— the test—
sending love spinning
out the door.

AFFECTION

Is a mental touch.
A continuous kiss.
Blowing in from lush islands.
Where palm trees wave.
And the sea breeze seeks
. . . nights descending
in sunshine.
Reigniting the cycle
of a dawning
warmth—
that endlessly arises
amidst sails
that never set.

BOWTIE BILLIONAIRES

We the people.
Of the people.
Love the people.
Hug the people.
Look up
to the people.
Look down
on the people.
Consider ourselves
one of the people.
People in.
And people out.
Peopling the place
with my people
and your people.
The people.
Those people.
People here.
People there.
People-people everywhere . . .
creating people power.
And power to the people.
Plus me,
feeling people's pain.

WORDLESS

That's speaking
from the grave.
As scarecrows weep.
And pigeons shit,
on my headstone.
Thinking . . .
they know me.
Drinking
to my health.
Like grave robbers
picking my brain.
And reusing my decay.
Like a skin graft
on bone . . .
to implant my soul
within themselves.
Like pacemakers
without a heart.

ROCK SOLID

She whispers from the trees.
Across the glen.
Calling me in . . .
snowbound.
Freezing.
Starving the light.
When a thaw strikes
and dawn begins . . .
beyond the storm.
Promising relief,
but delivering—
it all again.

FAMOUS WRITER

Drunken bastard.
Hiding in his house.
Acting large.
Dreaming the days
of our life.
But giving no credit.
Mere sympathy . . .
for the stick figures
he created
to face the music,
and play the band
by burying oneself
with his own spade
in a hole of royalties
cast upon the dead.

PAINTERS

It's all within reach.
Within touch.
But outside
the safety zone.
Which for some
is less
than an arm's length
away.
While the madness
starts at the fingertips.
Or is it
the vanishing point?
No, it's the sightlines
of the everyday
that must be captured
in colors of the spectrum,
or black and white.
Which is never
black nor white,
but off tones
. . . greys and such . . .
like moods
or shadows,
but it's exactly
this confusion

. . . or certainty . . .
that skews
the palates
of the mind . . .
while interpreting
concrete modernity
. . . or abstractions . . .
—constructing—
the current spirit,
or lay of the land.
Yet this rarely
pertains to realism;
naturalism,
and\or
daydreams
when not on canvas,
but against
the encompassing wall:
with signs posted
Artist
Beware
of interpreting:
what's not there.

GOLDEN GATE

Not meant to be romantic.
In the cold.
But it's California.
Sunshine and all.
But not here.
Not now.
Still when the winds
whip . . .
you think of brighter
days gone by.
Bringing a warmth
of realization . . .
it's not the weather
. . . it's the place.

MENTAL INTERCOURSE

A mind fuck—
some call it.
A brain bang.
It's the screw
without the mess.
Without the dinner,
date,
or kiss.
It's that time
you sat across the room
. . . in a church . . .
. . . or on a bus . . .
hell, it could've been
. . . when you . . .
were about to piss
yourself
outside the john
of that shithole bar,
and there they stood
—pretty as they please—
yours for the taking.
Theirs for the asking.
Needing only what . . .
you could give.
Taking only what . . .
you give away.
Everything in the moment.

161

The ravishing.
The romance.
The dreams.
And impossibilities.
It borders on lust,
but is so much more . . .
than a waking dream.
It's your entire life.
Condensed.
And growing.
No gloom.
Or shadows.
No hurt to others.
Or harm to yourself.
Nothing of the past.
With an orgasm
so physical
it extends beyond
thought.
To a reverie—
as coarse as rawhide
. . . or soft as goose down . . .
but as eternal
and burning
as the moment
you laid eyes
on all
. . . you wanted . . .
it to be.

WOODY

Idiots can't love.
Not truly.
And fuck the realist,
the worker bees,
the drones,
or farmers in the dell.
They don't know Monet
. . . the impressionist.
Or any kind'a jazz
—like Monk and Bird—
they're turd-worthless
in their bloodshot
eyes.
How can anyone
with dirty fingernails
and Budweiser smirks
touch the silken
breasts of maids
from the land
of milk and honey.
Where words,
gilded with gold,
fly like righteous angels—
healing the battle scars
of misanthropes,
and journeymen alike,
as they loathe

their aborted selves
for wasted years
—farming breadbaskets—
of the world
or roofing
family homes
with hammers
forged of steel
and knowledge
. . . not of numbers . . .
. . . or alternate possibilities . . .
to the vows
of real love and affection,
but only lessons learned
from the school of what
one sacrifices
to regenerate
an end
. . . *"esse "* . . .
that's honest
and true.

VIRGINAL

I'm banged-up
and bloated . . .
as depicted
on the back wall
of this dimly lit
church.
I should be speaking
French
but that's long past
a Vulgar Latin;
while I'm a refugee
from the Middle East,
but even they don't utter
my language
anymore.
Still I'm with child
and feel as stained
as the glass
encasing this place
most sacred.
But rarely
am I portrayed
as so . . .
especially not in art.
And hardly in word.

And most definitely
not in deed.
For I'm simply
a vessel.
A cathedral.
Or so they think.
The seed.
The egg.
But unbeknownst to them,
it's all me.
Gifted not from God,
but from the mother
I will always be.

HARE KRISHNA

Hare hare
. . . hare hare . . .
Where'd all that Krishna
go?
Dancing on
tippy-toes
like cannibals over
hot coals.
All swirly with love.
And oozing affection.
Smiles smitten
to their potato heads.
Wasn't this the want,
the need,
the end all
and be all . . .
for those who hate
God
. . . but adore
Peace and Love?
kṛṣṇa kṛṣṇa
. . . kṛṣṇa kṛṣṇa . . .

Isn't this the cling-clang
of scholarly speak—
what teachers insist?
Isn't this the campus?
The ethos . . .
of the Hollywood set?
And forget the Hamptons!
hare rāma
. . . hare rāma . . .
What no spandex!
And hairdos
are nonexistent.
rāma rāma
. . . hare hare . . .
With make-up,
being out
. . . and making-out . . .
a feral
emotion.
So idolatry
can't be spiritual
once you've seen the light
or attended a lecture
on climate change
or racism
or the evils
of waxing.

hare kṛṣṇa hare kṛṣṇa
kṛṣṇa kṛṣṇa hare hare
hare rāma hare rāma
rāma rāma hare hare
Let's not even talk
about gun control
or sex rights.
For laws
are lawless
and so unloving.
rāma rāma hare hare
That's the perfection
of Krishna!
Yet, shouldn't both
Hare and Rāma
be forever
condemned
to the same
altruistic
scrap heap
as all
the 60's . . . especially
the Summer
of Love.

WHITEIFIED

Black is black.
And white is white.
What a crock of shit.
Lies are the new white.
While black is a sham.
Or so the song goes . . .
do the hokey-pokey
and you turn them all around
. . . that's what it's all about.
Meaning truth
—our truth—
not yours
—ours—
where everything . . .
is as white
as fresh puss,
unless, it's your ghost.
Then it's the black
sheep of the family.
Something for slaughter
and the dankest
humor.
Like white lies
are no longer
black marks,

but the verity.
Placing the pistol
of purity
in our hands
and a bullet
between
. . . your lying eyes.

HI JACK

(A poem to Jack Kerouac)

Conned dreams beneath blubber boils
moaned bones smoked
tea toked
eyes bob in bloodshot sockets
no place to go
or groan
no place to die
only delays
answers away by the bay
anchors away my boy
bussed from Troy past goy
never would, couldn't could
nothing understood
never were
but remain, lovelorn stain
words on words the strain
lost eternal tomorrows
no sorrow, a sorrow
you thought would never come
then done, Kafka shunned
sad, sad past
sputter, sapped, a sap running, a running sap
addendum-all done-a-a-a-adam . . . Adam and
Eve
even atom you mean? A radioactive stream

atom-bombed, drunk adam's apple juice
ripple down a geek-necked sluice
smiles gone, miles gone
blue haired blond eyed boy conned
never was, just because
black polished hair boy fattened to forget
fattened for feast for tiny tease
rump-a-roast, rink-a-drink-a toast
insulated from ocean's spray
go away, go away, what's to say today
yesterday
poetry none no more, never got there
word scratched whore, thick-tongued bore
got what's coming, fell down running
skipped a town, shoe shine brown
look around, football clown
everybody boarded and departs
all stops no starts
lacky-whacky stokes the train of endless
destinations
steam pressed, done, everyone thanking God
pure faced girl next door is dead
or never was
thought warped scuzz
a darkness has puffed you out
all red-cold and bloated
floated, babble, steel wheel rabble
smokestacked coals and
piggy backs

communist, hip-no-tits and caddy-lacks
ransacks, meat racks, hacks on tracks
taxied and factzied, no pure bred blacks
bourbon puffed wisdom from frosted lips
spittle, a final frost edged tip
cigar croaked bloke a joke
a laughing lion broke, where's the roar
pearls of wisdom on the floor
a toothless earl, a low-well drown duke
marshmallow fruitcakes, success a fluke
heaven takes, for lordy shakes
good-God-ies break
barnyard scared we pick your bones
heads shake who knows no groans, yes and no
nothing drawn tight, no rope they hold
rooms a darkie, drapes a shut
only cord for window shades do pull
unknotted
untied
untried
crucified
nail in hands
that's the plan
hand in hand
you climb the cross
nothing lost
no tight rope noose
nothing loose

just 100 proof
everything purged
mortgage secured, car loan owed
not is not not, only knot
where did you go artist?
no such thing critics sing
flight of fancy
on the wing
gone we fear all
nothing rolls nothing now
no bar stall wake-up calls
no autumn fall foot-a-ball
morgues a staffed, puff huff shirt collar stuff
pancake make-up
life-long break-up
cabbie squawk, dovetailed hawks, nothing
walks
every-one knows, nothing new
no new to you or you or you
ice turned blue hue and you who too
a blue hue you hue
blew you boo-boo
then no go below you
pallid salad, skin shrink, inky-dink, no pink
stinky-stink
worm meat, all treat, sold books what's the
hook?
worm-meat that's the beat
retreat, deedy-deat, milkless teat

dried out meat
beat no more my baby
oh, beat no more today
roads lead down a foxhole
only six feet away
say
thanks Jack, for the yakety-yack.

SUN SHINES IN A LIBRARY

Drunks find tanning beneath
the skylight's sun
a place of warmth
and food for thought.
Where reading is an addiction
but no antidote
. . . for the high . . .
that knowledge nurtures—
for the sober
who say . . .
there by the grace
of God
go I.

UP IN SMOKE

Like long legs
that extend
to heaven
—knows where—
it's there
it fades
and disappears.
Same with sex
Only the deed
leaves a heat
that flows
like whiskey.
Stumbling the senses . . .
with straight shots.
Pour after pour
. . . until the match
is lit again.

THE BASTARD LIFE

What the fuck's wrong
with me?
I've lived the bastard life
because I believed
in divine intervention
and the uniqueness
of the Self;
by being an imbecile
who suckled
on the pap
that we're all unique
inside . . .
with a special gift.
Even the prick
. . . philosophers . . .
peddled this shit.
Leaving no escape
for me
as I walled myself in,
remaining true
to my Cause,
untouched.
Pure to the bone.
Destructively iconoclastic.
As I awaited my—
earthly resurrection.
My applause.

And acknowledgement.
Oh sure . . .
the true believers
roared and clapped
at my All-American
athleticism
and business acumen,
but stood shocked
and awed
when I walked
away.
Continuing along,
the novelistic road
to my bastard life.
Where a published novel
was to bring my voice . . .
to the world.
Along with my delusional dreams
of universal conversations . . .
when only crickets
erupted in reply.
Stopping me cold.
At my path's end.
Facing the abyss
of my heartfelt idiocy.
When a mucky
little side route
. . . running parallel . . .

to my bastard life—
poetically appeared.
Stripping bare
I plunged ahead.
Dirty, filthy,
gloriously at ease.
Saved by—
my own hand.
While still unscathed
by any divinity
or its bastard ways.

DIVORCE

Finally!
I've waited all my life
for its arrival.
Posters and stories
of earlier shows
thrilled me.
With a circus
of dreams—
and expectations.
Plus the chills
of what's to come.
Creating a storybook.
Complete
with the whimsical
reverberations
of life's calliopes
heralding forth
the strongmen . . .
and women . . .
as beautiful
as bridesmaids
who celebrate
the raising
of the main pole.
Lifting the Big Top
skyward.

With the cosmic power
of corn popping.
And elephants trumpeting.
While monkeys cheered
through clownish grins.
Everything exhilarating
past the anticipations
of lifelong dreams.
Spinning sweetness
like cotton candy . . .
all pink with possibility
of adults
melding into children
and back again.
Mastering the ring
like circling stallions.
Wedded to a band
of like-minded mares.
When high above
as the wires tighten
. . . out step artists . . .
like angels in white.
Willowy as fairy
princesses
and muscular
as men of steel . . .
groomed from the heavens.

When a once
in lifetime
—trapeze—
kisses the clouds.
All gasping.
One two three!
As together—
they dare the devil.
As eyes affix . . .
on the coupling.
And throats croak
in anticipation
of every catch
and release.
With unassailable
coordination
and trust . . . becoming
the safety net itself.
Until one hand slips.
Or the other forgets.
Taking for granted
the grasp
and connection.
Clutching only air.
Shattering . . .
all the funhouse mirrors.
Freeing every lion, tiger
and bear.

While emptying the tent
and filling
the wishing well
with plug nickels,
unusable,
unredeemable,
at the ticket booths
—of events—
never to come again.

PLAID

Short plaid skirts—
that run up the poles
of milk white skin . . .
are the surrender flags
of dirty old men.
Akin to kilts
of antiquity
one supposes.
But that's just . . .
an impotency.
Forgotten.
Lost.
Like the basics
of belief
in true Gods
and holy ghost.
And ancestors . . .
still surviving . . .
amongst the clouds.
When hunting
meant survival
and family
was sustenance,
itself.
And sex
was a necessity,

a continuation,
an antidote,
to disease
and death.
In childbirth
or on the battlefield
there's something that—
plaid buntings
once denoted.
But sadly . . .
has vaporized
in a jumble of thoughts
that border on chastity,
but disintegrate
with decline
. . . like the laughter
of a young girl fading
—into a love—
in spousal form.
Entombing
the recollection
in the deleterious
melancholy . . .
of ridiculousness.

DRUNKEN POETS

Why?
Because they have to.
Except for Emily.
The rest
gott'a exit
stage left
or right
no matter.
There's no vacation.
Only getaways.
Where words
run free
and the masses
consent
to revelations
most majestic.
With inner visions
. . . so inhumanly . . .
impossible to conceive . . .
it's all a daydream
— a most dangerous trance—
for the bard
who wallows
in this marsh
like a moonstruck
child.

Until the sun rises
and sobriety sets in.
Fading the reverie.
Back to the falseness
of words.
And the pettiness
of the attempt.

GIRLS

They got a treasure
that no boys know.
At least not originally
. . . but the flame . . .
. . . the thing . . .
takes hold.

SOCIAL NETWORKING

It's all a short-change
artist.
Taking the hardest earned
and giving only . . .
vapor back.
But that's not a crime
or even a sin.
It's the future
and past.
Never . . .
becoming the present.
That's the robbery.
A collective theft
with its pictures
of places
seen and forgotten . . .
other than as pot shots
of places
seen and forgotten
or remembered
like it was yesterday
. . . even if the snap
was taken instantly
—it's old—
buried in the moment.
Silent as a grave.

If it speaks
its gibbering history
about a morrow . . .
that's only a repeat
of treadmills
going nowhere.
Losing nothing.
Gaining nothing.
Except a sum zero.
With the Now only—
realized
in the arms of love . . .
from first sight.
To the initial kiss
of an end
. . . that breaks . . .
not hearts,
but the ice
within.

SLOPPY SECONDS

It's only . . .
a man's world.
A way of life
for some dudes.
Taking what's left
is all they get.
Or want.
While others
ride roughshod
over
those not grabbing
. . . the prize
. . . on the first spin
of the merry-go-round.
Strange.
But the brass ring
is always there
for the taking.
But some don't reach.
Others miss.
Leaving a group
of two
with one
desperately lusting
for the reward—

but deeply fearing
its demands.
Or considerations.
And the other
not caring
for the concerns
of the first.
Only taking
what is rightfully
his.
That in a nutshell
is the long
and short
of a man's
world.

MONEY

Does buy.

KITSCH

Is free love.
All hugs.
And kisses.
To the smallest
of furry animals
with adorable eyes
. . . that laugh
out loud
or cry
for sympathy . . .
before star-studded
studios
of mass appeal.
Where news
is the punchline
and narcissism
so delectably hip
that sunshine
bounces
about the beds
of roses . . .
with the light
and airiness
of a childhood
dream.
Breeding
fantasies

of the world's
most powerful
being . . . place . . .
or thing.
Becoming one
with me
and mine.
Exact opposite
of art's indifference—
that demands
a flow
from the oversoul
of human nature.
Tested and true
. . . with . . .
everlasting questions
and comforts
written in stone
or carved
from marble
. . . painted
on kaleidoscopes
of past,
present,
and future lives.
Finding no human
idolatry
in the heart

of Its everlasting
presence . . .
that shuns
every "ism"
except
the one
unvarnished
by self-perpetuation—
allowing
only a personal honesty.
Wistfully.
Seeking . . .
death-defying
truths.

SPINNING

(A NON-POEM)

Every Saturday
I provide
protective muscle
to my beautiful,
almond eyed,
wife
as she walks
to her cult
of aerobicized
yogi dancers
. . . situated
smack dab
in our toilet
of a neighborhood.
And there
. . . at the only newspaper box . . .
left unmolested
by looters
and other denizens
of this Boschian
dream
I buy my
San Francisco Chronicle.

When three weeks ago
this Saturday,
the freakin' ghost
of Ho Chi Minh
. . . had he . . .
. . . lost the war . . .
and indulged
in America's
peace pipe
of homelessness
and street life . . .
stood pathetically bent
in his off-white
trench coat
caked in yesterday's
gastronomical
evacuations
. . . smack dab . . .
before the piss yellow
dispensary
of worldly bullshit
—examining—
through the shattered
plastic
glass
how socially responsible
people
live and work.

When to my astonishment,
he actually started grubbing
through a bag
so soiled . . .
it looked like it cleaned
the bottom
of his bum's feet . . .
when what to my wondering eyes
should appear
but multiple,
immaculately,
shiny coins
. . . being shoved
. . . in the slot
as the fucking—
idiot bastard
stole
the last
of my news.

POTUS

Once
when France
witnessed
a girly frog
turn into
a soldier . . .
it arched
the world
towards
a warrior
like me.
Divining
my presence
with an inbred
blamelessness.
Born
beyond
peasantry
and divided sects.
To reign
with the divinity
of my pastor's
righteous
dream . . .
of fathers
praised
so heavenly

by sons
—with a ghostlike—
chance
of conquering
hopelessness
—through my—
most sacred struggle
. . . assailing . . .
my envisioning
—away from wars
of a hundred
years—
or Reichs
where
false prophets
narcissistically
scribble
the solution
while I
wave a flag
of time
where strife
was feudal
and royals
rich as kings
swiftly striking
my ascension
with swords

so barbarously
concentrated
they camp
within
my heart
. . . bleeding me . . .
to a bloodlessness
that brings my
battle
to an end.
Not—
as a mortal man
or brother
of a race's kin
. . . but a . . .
destiny's child
surrounded
by chorales
of archangels
and sisters
so celestially
strong
they sing
the walk
of fame . . .
in manifestos
of gold.

And books
so eternal
they constantly
recall
my name
"intelligentsia."
Not the illiterate
victim
of a continent's
blackest
death . . .
but float
upon my flame
rising
like a mystic
high
above
the murderous stake
where I take . . .
my rightful place.

A CHILD'S BURBLING

In public
it's verse.
A strangled poem.
A self-anthem.
Extending to the world
but not caring
about relating
. . . unless you've got
the answer . . .
or a cookie.
Oh, you can join
in the fun
but not
the discourse.

HEMINGSTEIN

Found prose
in a pounding
hard-on.
But the blood
that pumped
and flowed
was stiffened
with shots
of bloodied
Marys
infused
with a honeyed
blond . . .
of oysters
sans the pearl . . .
chilled
and shaken
by world events
that plucked
straw-haired boys
from trout streams
. . . to partake
of battlefields
ablaze

with hybrid
men
pieced together
like puzzles
with missing parts.
Except . . .
for the women
and children
and bits
of pets
mixed
in the blood
and brain
of a continent
gone insane
—like an embryonic fluid—
so mind-boggling . . .
man could only birth
a fiction
of himself.
One struck dumb by
the speechlessness
of worlds
at war.
Much like that
. . . of the sexes . . .
where everything
is a minefield

and trench warfare
is hand-to-hand
combat—
fought with pillows
and flowers.
Drunk with wine.
And a carnal ideology
that pits family
against fun
and saintliness
over promiscuity.
Forcing the subversive
and\or
adventurous . . .
to bury the romantics
in the salt-of-the-earth.

GENEROSITY

Of spirit
rivals love.
Generosity
of spirit
is immediate giving—
to strangers
and the world.
Generosity
of spirit
is a flow
so personal
it embarrasses
the recipient
or stuns them
silly.
Mesmerizes, maybe.
It's both seeing
and feeling
an existing chi
of the giver's
generosity
of spirit—
being a comfort zone
. . . so huge . . .
it embraces
cats and kitties

of all makes,
models,
and sizes.
Generosity
of spirit
melts hot
with a coolness
so sublime
it alters the forces. . .
of nature . . .
with a humanism
so unique
and individual
it can't be exchanged
or replicated
or bound
to a gospel,
or political party,
or the rationalization
of private wants
and needs.
Generosity
of spirit
is a gift
to the witness
free
of charge.

DRUG FREE

Illegal—
but free of charge!
At the Man's Warehouse.
On the street corner
of NO
and RETURN.
Where it's limitless . . .
blow, baby
or Beat, Blue Heavens.
Mercy, mercy me.
NoSireee, you Blotters.
It's government sanctioned.
On the taxpayers' tab.
And free for all.
It's the end
of the war on drugs.
It's the hostel . . .
for China Girls,
Georgia Homeboys,
and your Aunt Hazel.
Baby, baby, oh baby.
It's a roadhouse.
A boarding house.
It's an industrial-sized
Trap House . . .
called Satan's Secret.
Or the Speedball Express.
A place that's nationwide.

One you can eternally . . .
check into.
But never leave.
It's Fritos, Fruit Loops
and Ding Dongs galore.
Flat screens and X-Boxes
to your heart's content.
And as unrestricted . . .
as any Special K.
Just like the sex,
it's all recreational
and free
for the asking.
Or taking.
With Wolfies
by the handful
and Mollies all the rave.
Turning angels
into dust
and men
into Mary Janes.
But no matter . . .
what the Tweek
or how blue
—the devils become—
there's no In and Out
policy.
There's only the—
law-abiding IN

. . . initiative . . .
of a drug free
America!
Creating a smorgasbord
of all you can ingest
and sweet Jesus
. . . my dearly addicted . . .
there ain't no exit.
No way out.
No door to freedom.
Only pots of Beans
and fryers of Ope.
And rehab?
Furgit'a'bout'it!
Rehab?
Rehab is an OD
or bullet.
Meaning . . .
my dearest hooked
and wasted . . .
escape is in a box
or body bag—
*for all societies '
misunderstood.*
With the check-out time
. . . being the moment . . .
the good times rolled.
Unconditionally.
And you partied
free of charge.

EASY RIDERS

PEACE-SEX-DRUGS
Now, that's what it was supposed to be
PEACE-SEX-DRUGS
Now, that's what it was
PEACE-SEX-DRUGS
Now, that's what?
PEACE-SEX-DRUGS.

GAY

For those on the outside
it's a double layered bubble.
It's all perfectly clear.
Similar
and connected
by the same old things.
Yet there's a separation
of air . . .
of space . . .
the bubble lifts
with a sigh—
when it's expected
to tumble.
Or threatens to burst.
Instead of contracting.
It's the same air
on the inside
as the out,
but the surface tension
has a different quake
and shiver.
Unalike in the light
while shining—
the selfsame rainbow
on the outer skin.

Yet spinning ...
in a different direction.
Rising and falling
on the current breeze.
Seeking the still
or a crossing wind.
Yet the urge to poke
or catch it gently
on the palm
is both a delight
and bane.
As confusingly ...
natural
as venturing into a mystery
with something
... you've known ...
all your life.

PURE VANITY

Infection.
Scabies.
Typhus.
The truncheon.
A whip . . .
that burns
the flesh . . .
in gas ovens
and death chambers
ENDED
when we ripped
the guard apart
and fed Its heart
to the shepherd
who . . .
we then bludgeoned
to death
and heaped Its carcass
on the ash
of our mothers
and sisters.
Some three weeks ago
. . . today . . .
when we staggered
and crawled
on the knees
of animals—

218

towards the Commandant
and his soon to be—
executioner
who handed us
chocolate and crackers
and the bread of life
. . . a smile . . .
topped with the warmest
of garnishes
a hug, maybe,
if our stink
and depravity
wasn't too strong
. . . leading us like desiccated
cows
to barns
where they powdered
our noses
with DDT
stripping us
of our pearl necklaces
of well-fed lice,
but no need for a mirror.
We were all reflections
of one another.
The spitting image
of our starvation diet.
But slowly we took food
and water

and our scarecrow forms
began to take shape.
But stalled.
No matter . . .
the amount of medicine.
Or rest.
When a doctor
in a medical gown
took note
of rouge red
no longer
only rimming
. . . wounds . . .
but tinting the lips
and cheeks
of the healthier
—faster recovering—
feline queens
. . . like a miracle cure . . .
he sequestered
—from the local—
. . . partners in crime . . .
clothes
and shoes,
plus, any trinket
or two of whimsy.
Of fashion.
Humming, humming, humming
like inmates

awaiting release,
if not, full pardons.
Excited yet tremulous
at the thought
of redressing
a general population
... as a whole ...
while rewriting
a timeless prescription
—that once destroyed—
Adorn Thyself!
Remaking oneself ...
in a beauty
so radiant ...
that the deathlessness
of spirit ...
becomes a feast
for the eyes.

MENAGES A TROIS

Are so murderously indecisive.
There's a giving and a taking
of half-lives.
The same dilemma—
as identical twins.
With everything being
perfectly the same
on the outside.
But one is older
and the other
perpetually newer.
Meaning wisdom,
opposed to youthfulness,
is the norm.
The excitement.
The infinite growth.
Then along—
comes the triplet
and the two poles
attracting,
or repelling,
spinning north
and south,
lustfully . . .
finding their bearing
. . . creating the heat
of convention

222

and the electricity
of love.
Becomes neither
one way or the other.
Thus spiking the compass
to paradise
with no true direction.
Only the wait
and see.
As the opposing poles
. . . and those attracting . . .
keep the spin alive
or pull it to a dead stop.
The friction
of seeking equilibrium
in unison with a positive
and negative
—fragments—
the laws of nature
. . . no matter how much . . .
the magnetism,
because a half rotation,
forward and back,
back and forward,
creates a positive
over the negative.
Or the vice . . . of versa . . .
leaving only one way to go.
Away.
In a never-ending circle.

223

EYES

Until the face
was lifted
the eyes were a sight
unseen.
Too startling
to be beautiful.
Too shocking
to sustain a dream.
But ending
at their openings
. . . turns a majestic act . . .
to a skeletal wake.
While linked
via flesh and bone
to a body
designed to take.
Possess
and own.
Yet the color
is no gemstone . . .
as it goes without a tint
. . . but a transparency
so crystal clear
—they'd freeze ice—
with a single glint.

Chilling the hostage
too dearly
to look away,
but terrified
of peering
—straight in—
witnessing a ruby mass
of mindfulness . . .
that observes nothing . . .
when it comes to you.

FATHERHOOD

Deployment begins
with the preordained
sighting
of prey . . .
while recording
the landscape's
ups and downs
beyond the immediate
backdrop . . .
of potential escape routes
and places to hide.
All forming the paths
of attack
by setting the bait
and springing the trap
that rains rings of gold
and arrows of affection
down on the
encircled . . .
in a courtship
of lust
cloaked
in the commitment
of love.
When this end result
. . . of all the feasting . . .
vows from birth

to replay the hunt.
Only this time . . .
with the new
and varied
methods of evolution
. . . that transcend
anything
not involved—
in the physical feeding
and incubation
of that Being formed.
Both inside and outside
the fleshy walls
of maternity.
Leaving only,
a distant sense
of participation.
One that knows . . .
only herding
or stalking.
Making all the flock
jittery
or confusingly aware
of the hunter
in their midst.
One that knows both
. . . the power of the bow
and the potential
within the quiver.

Driving him back
to the blind . . .
so as not to spook
the ever-maturing prey
. . . he so pridefully
observes as man's
future provider.
Or the selfsame sheep
as he—
never truly partaking
of the green
. . . from either side . . .
of the fence.

THE THERMONUCLEAR SHIELD
OF A NIGHT CLUB

Rhythm and Blues
is supposed to be . . .
the clarion call
for the demilitarized zone
of diverseness.
As the drums pound
an opening shot
and the bass beats
. . . towards the bottom . . .
of the soul.
A guitarist guns
the engine
and a singer steps to the mike
as the house fills
with the smoke
of anticipation
—when an enemy—
—within—
entrenched behind a battlement
of booze
and entitlement
contests the pending conquest
with the sound
of his own voice.
Rising off key
to the troopers

on stage.
At first, the incursion is ignored.
Hoping for a retreat
in the wake
of what's understood.
But the assault continues.
Growing louder.
And more persistent.
As the music fails
to beat back
his pounding
narcissism.
Not even . . .
the collective sense
of troops
most loyal
to the headliners
. . . and nobodies alike . . .
can end the intrusion.
Until a foot soldier
for the devotees
—of the performance—
begins to hatch
a counter attack
on the invasive boor
. . . of the night . . .
. . . of the club . . .
of the musical congregation.

He intuitively recruits:
The Suit,
The Beret,
and dreaded Porkpie.
Or the cloth helmet
in Turban form.
All juxtaposing the draft
of the Cowboy Hat . . .
so solidly conscripted
. . . to confront
the "Assaultive"
with a counter offensive
—that's nearing zero hour—
as the lead singer,
the front man,
begins to launch an anthem
—the powder keg—
that rocks the roll.
When in like time,
the self-appointed
legionnaire
unhesitatingly homes in
on his enemy's flank
. . . preparing his assault
. . . for the faithful.
When through
the candle lit gloom . . .
of a perfectly manicured night
—gone wrong—

a bejeweled hand
appears swan-like
from the portending mist
of conflict.
And with a single touch
. . . most feminine . . .
falls melodiously upon
Its shoulder
—stunning the creature—
as all goes silent
along the battle front
of gratitude
and appreciation
. . . victoriously . . .
recapturing the room.

The End

A

B

C

N

O

P

R

S

T

U

V

W

Also by Peter Jacob Streitz:

No Words ... Just News (poetry)

No Church Nor Pew (poetry)

Past Oz... Land of the Misbegotten (novel)

Peter's books are available through Amazon

https://www.facebook.com/PeterJStreitz

https://www.bluepiscespress.com

Made in the USA
Columbia, SC
19 July 2023

20411465R00137